The PAN AMERICAN UNION

JOHN BARRETT : : Director General
FRANCISCO J. YANES : Assistant Director

YERBA MATE : THE TEA OF SOUTH AMERICA

Reprinted from the May, 1916, issue of the Bulletin of the Pan American Union - - - Washington, D. C.

WASHINGTON
GOVERNMENT PRINTING OFFICE
1916

In the interest of creating a more extensive selection of rare historical book reprints, we have chosen to reproduce this title even though it may possibly have occasional imperfections such as missing and blurred pages, missing text, poor pictures, markings, dark backgrounds and other reproduction issues beyond our control. Because this work is culturally important, we have made it available as a part of our commitment to protecting, preserving and promoting the world's literature. Thank you for your understanding.

YERBA MATE--THE TEA OF SOUTH AMERICA[1]

MAN, primitive or cultured, seems to be so constituted that he needs, or imagines he needs, periodically or regularly and habitually administered, some kind of a stimulant or narcotic—and he generally manages to get it. That, too, whether he lives in the wilds of Africa, in the heart of India, on the banks of the Euphrates, or in the crowded capitals of Europe and the Americas. An African tribe may be so low in the scale of human intelligence that its members can count no farther than 3, but some of them will have found a way to prepare from some vegetable substance an alcoholic liquor that will exhilarate, excite, and generally intoxicate, even as their paler brothers of the highest intellect and culture have discovered how to make champagne and various other liquid refreshments that cheer and also inebriate.

The stimulant, or narcotic, may not always be in the form of a liquid, for sometimes it is smoked, as is the opium of the Chinese, or that most cherished of all weeds, tobacco; and again it may be eaten, as is that sweetened preparation of hemp leaves, known as *bhang*, in its Turkish form called *hashish*. Whatever the name or form or method devised for taking it into the human system, the effects produced are more or less alike; and the worst feature of all these intoxicating inventions of man is that they are habit-forming in their effects and invariably lead to intemperance in their use. Fortunately, however, there are a few products of nature that, when properly prepared, will largely satisfy this craving for exhilaration or stimulation without inducing intoxication and without the injurious effects attendant upon the use of the more powerful drinks and drugs above alluded to.

Among the various harmless stimulants whose effects are really beneficial there are two beverages which are of strictly American origin, the plants which produce them being indigenous to the Americas, and the drink prepared from them having been invented and concocted by the aborigines long before the Columbian discovery. One of these, a well-known food and drink as well as mild stimulant, has been dealt with heretofore in an article on Theobroma Cacao—or chocolate. The other is not so well known throughout the world, although it is the favorite beverage of perhaps 15,000,000 people in South America; it is called *yerba mate* in the Spanish-speaking countries, *herva matte* in Brazil, and Paraguayan tea elsewhere in the world.

[1] By Edward Albes, of Pan American Union staff.

GATHERING YERBA MATÉ.

Left: Leaves of the *Ilex paraguayensis*—the yerba maté tree. Center: The native gatherer, variously called *yerbatero*, *tarifero*, or *minero*, at work with his machete hacking off the smaller branches and leaves of the tree. Right: Carrying the cut branches and leaves, by means of the *diza*, or strip of hide, which is passed around the forehead, the ends being tied to the bundle whose weight is distributed on the shoulders and back.

The term *yerba mate*, since it is used to denote the plant as well as the drink, may need some little explanation in order to avoid a confusion of terms in the following sketch. The Guarani Indians, who first made known the plant and the use of its leaves to the Spaniards in Paraguay and to the Portuguese in southern Brazil, call it *caa*—the plant—that is the plant that is unique among all others, *the* plant of all plants, so to speak. *Caa guazu*, the more specific term, meant the "big" or "splendid plant." The Spaniards, translating literally, called it *yerba*—the herb. The *mate*—Spanish for gourd—came to be used in connection with *herba* because it was in a dried gourd that the pulverized leaves were steeped in boiling water to prepare the drink. By habit the container began to imply the contents and *yerba*, the herb, and *mate*, the gourd, combined meant the gourd-herb, and became the name of the plant and then of the drink made therefrom.

The plant, known botanically as *Ilex Paraguayensis*, is the South American holly, and is indigenous to a large scope of country embracing the four Brazilian States of Paraná, Santa Catharina, Rio Grande do Sul, and Matto Grosso; the northern section of Argentina; and the eastern and central portions of Paraguay. It is an evergreen tree or shrub which grows from 12 to 26 feet in height, very bushy and beautiful and from a distance looking much like an orange tree. The leaves are a glossy green, the flowers small and yellowish in color, and the little berries a purplish black. Some varieties, especially those having a small leaf of dark green shade, are preferred because they are said to make the finest quality of tea. The fruit is attached to the branches by a short stalk and contains a soft pulp in which are imbedded four little hard seeds.

These seeds, when left exposed for a few days, get so dry and hard that it takes a sharp knife to cut them. As a result, all efforts to propagate the plants from seeds failed for many years, as they invariably refused to germinate. The Jesuit fathers in southern Brazil, however, were a very observant and thoughtful class of men. They found that the plant in its native forests was propagated chiefly from seeds that had passed through the digestive tract of birds that had eaten the berries, the intestinal juices having first softened the hard shell of the seed, so that when deposited on the ground the strength of the embryo within was sufficient to burst its covering and germination was made easy. The shrewd fathers forthwith devised a method of chemically treating the seeds to accomplish the same result artificially, and thus successfully started the first yerba mate plantations. The method of preparing the seeds was not divulged by the Jesuits, however, and when they were later expelled from Brazil the industry of cultivating herva in plantations was entirely abandoned. In recent years, however, new experiments have met with success, and

CARRYING THE PRODUCT TO THE CAMP.

The branches and leaves are gathered in great piles and at the end of the day's work are carried in the manner shown above to the camp to undergo the curing process outlined in the text.

there are now a number of flourishing plantations in Parana, Brazil, as well as in Paraguay.

Starting a *yerba mate* plantation is not so simple and easy a matter as might be supposed. The young plant is rather tender and sensitive, and needs in its early stages abundant shade. The seed is therefore usually sown in forest land, where the surrounding vegetation furnishes the needed protection until the plant has developed sufficiently to withstand the heat of the direct rays of the sun. The surrounding shrubs and trees are then cleared away and the well-started plant begins to thrive. One result of cultivating the mate tree is that when given unrestricted sunshine and open air it spreads out its branches and becomes bushy, thus producing more and better leaves than does the wild tree, which is often hampered by its environment, and while drawn upward to greater heights in order to reach the light and air it needs, has a much smaller spread and fewer branches and leaves. Some cultivators have adopted the method of sowing the seeds of the rapidly growing castor-oil plant in close proximity to the yerba mate seedlings, the former much more quickly developed plant furnishing the required shade for as long as it is needed.

Another characteristic of the yerba tree is that of its adaptability to its environment, such as accommodating itself to different soils and varying degrees of moisture. The wild species is usually found along the low shores of rivers, where it has a superabundance of moisture; but it has been found that the cultivated varieties will flourish about as well on higher ground having natural or artificial drainage, and need no artificial watering. The zone of cultivation, therefore, may be greatly extended, and eventually reach far beyond the tree's present natural habitat. In the future, as the world's demand for yerba mate increases, the plantation product will doubtless replace that of the native forests, for the cultivated groves once established, the crop is more easily gathered and with far less expense. In the meantime, the old method of gathering, drying, and powdering the leaves of the forest product still prevails in most of the sections which now supply the world's demand, and may be outlined as follows:

The native gatherers usually go into the forests in small companies or groups under the leadership of a manager or overseer, who is generally an expert in the work of gathering and preparing the yerba leaves and at the same time knows how to manage his men to advantage. Having selected a place where the trees are plentiful and within easy walking distance, a camp is made. The leaves must be gathered at their early maturity and when the weather is dry, so the time for the work is usually about the beginning of May. Temporary quarters are first erected, consisting of sheds covered with the broad leaves of palms or of banana trees.

Courtesy of Señor Alfonso Guerdile, Buenos Aires.

A BARBACUA FOR PREPARING YERBA.

The first consideration in the treatment of the maté is to effect its cure, as it may be called, by scorching immediately after the branches and leaves are collected. It is then taken to the *barbacuá* for final curing.

MATÉ GATHERING, AT A FOREST DEPOT, PARANA.

The mode of living and the habits of the yerbateros differ only slightly in all parts where the maté grows. These huts and hide sacks of the prepared tea are seen in Brazil as well as in Paraguay.

While some of the men are engaged in this work another squad is busily engaged in constructing what is known as the *tatacua*. This is a small plot of ground, about 6 feet square, which is beaten down and pounded with heavy wooden mallets until its surface becomes firm and hard. At the four corners are driven large stakes, while upon the smoothed surface are piled logs of wood, which later serve for fuel. It is at this place that the leaves and small twigs are collected and placed in huge piles by the gatherers for their first scorching, the fired logs furnishing the required heat. After this first scorching the leaves are stripped from the smallest branches and twigs, and, being collected in large square nets made of strips of hide, are taken to another place called the *barbacua*.

The *barbacua* consists of a large arch supported on three trestles, the center trestle being the highest. The roof of the arch consists of a superstructure of crosspieces nailed to stakes on either side of the central supports. The leaves are then spread out on this roof and a hot fire kindled underneath. Several of the workers are stationed about the structure, armed with long poles, to prevent ignition of the leaves. When the leaves have become thoroughly cured and dried, a process which consumes about 24 hours, the fire underneath is extinguished and the ground carefully swept and cleaned and then pounded with the great mallets until the surface is smooth and almost as hard as stone. The cured leaves are then thrown down from the roof, and by means of a rudely constructed mill are pulverized.

The *tatacua* and *barbacua* having been prepared, the gathering squads proceed to the places where the yerba trees are found in greatest profusion. They grow irregularly, sometimes only a few to an acre and occasionally in large clumps from which a bounteous harvest is easily procured. About the only implements with which each gatherer is supplied are a machete or a small ax, a kind of leather hopple called *manea*, which, when tied to both ankles, serves as an aid to climbing the trees, and a wide strap or strip of hide, called *alza*, which is passed around the forehead, the ends being tied to the great bundles of branches and leaves, to be carried on the shoulders and back. This method of portage, distributing the weight carried between the shoulders and on the back, leaving the hands and arms free, seems to be a favorite one among the natives of many of the countries of South America.

In gathering the leaves the *yerbatero*, or gatherer, climbs the tree and hacks off all the smaller leaf-bearing branches, leaving the tree practically denuded. Left undisturbed for about three years, the tree develops new branches and leaves, and another supply is ready for a new harvest. The branches and leaves are gathered in huge piles, and at the end of the day's work are carried in the manner outlined above to the camp to undergo the curing and pulverizing process.

After the leaves have been pulverized the next step is that of packing the product for shipment. The native method is packing the powdered yerba into hide sacks. The half of a raw oxhide is sewed together in the form of a square sack, one side or end being left open. Two of the corners are then strongly tied to two strong stakes driven deep into the ground, and the pulverized product is packed and pounded down into the sack by means of a large pestle made of a stout staff, with a heavy wooden block at the end. When filled to its utmost capacity, the sack is sewed up, and after it is exposed to the sun for a day or two the hide dries out and the bundle becomes as dense and hard almost as stone. The filled sacks weigh from 200 to 220 pounds each, and in this state are ready for shipment and export. They are transported on mule back or by means of oxcarts to the distributing centers and seaports.

The methods outlined above are those which have obtained in Paraguay and southern Brazil for centuries. In recent years, however, more modern and improved methods of curing, pulverizing, and packing the product have been introduced, and the number of *mate* mills is constantly increasing. In the State of Paraná, Brazil, there are now something over 30 improved *mate* mills, called *engenhos*, half of them being in Curityba, the capital of the State, whence large quantities are annually exported to Argentina, Uruguay, Chile, Bolivia, and some even to European countries. The value of the *mate* exported by the Brazilian States of Paraná, Santa Catharina, and Rio Grande do Sul amounts annually to about $8,727,000. In 1915 the imports of Argentina of yerba mate from Brazil amounted to about 48,000 tons and from Paraguay about 3,500 tons.

As to *yerba mate*, the beverage, it may be well, in order to avoid confusion with the plant, to call it Paraguayan tea. As intimated above, it was the favorite beverage and stimulant of the Guarani Indians for many years before the Spanish conquest of Paraguay and the Portuguese settlement of Brazil. They taught the use of it to the Jesuit fathers, who soon recognized its virtues and made the collection and preparation of the product an important industry, establishing quite a number of large and flourishing plantations, which became the centers for their great missionary work among the natives.

The Indians prepared the drink by placing a small quantity of the powdered leaves in a receptacle, usually a clean, dried gourd from which the stem had been cut—thus leaving a round aperture at the top—and then pouring in very hot or boiling water. After being allowed to steep for a few minutes, a little lemon juice or perhaps some sweet substance was added and the decoction was ready for consumption. Since the small particles of the leaves would not

From an old engraving in a book of travels over Paraguay, published in England, 1839.

PROCESS OF PREPARING THE YERBA.

The leaves and small twigs are first smoked and even scorched in a place where they are exposed to a fire smoldering beneath them. This is called a *tatacua*.

Courtesy of Señor Alfonso Guerdile, Buenos Aires.

A BARBACUA AND THE YERBATEROS.

After the first process of scorching the twigs and leaves at the *tatacua* is completed, they are gathered and taken to the next curing place, the *barbacuá*, where the curing process is completed, as outlined in the text.

settle to the bottom, it had been found necessary to invent a tube having some kind of strainer at the end through which the liquid might be sucked from the receptacle. A short piece of cane, or perhaps the upper bone of the wing of a large bird, with one end covered with a bulb of closely woven fiber served the purpose for the natives. This implement was given the name of *bombilla*—little pump—by the Spaniards, who later improved it by making it of metal, the tube having a perforated, spoon-shaped end that served to stir as well as to strain the liquid.

Among the Indians it was the custom and for that matter is yet, when the stranger entered their camp or communal hut, to forthwith prepare a gourd of *yerba mate*. The beverage being ready for consumption, the chief or head man would take a sip through the *bombilla* and then pass the receptacle to the visitor, who was expected to partake thereof in the same manner and through the same tube. It was then passed on from one to another until all present had partaken, when it was started on another round, and so on until the supply was exhausted. To refuse to sip through the same *bombilla* is regarded as unpardonable rudeness and even an insult. The custom of the host taking the first sip originated no doubt in the intention to assure the guest that the potion was not poisoned and that he was safe among them. That this custom is still observed, not only among the natives but also among the settlers of European descent in the remote districts, is evidenced by the following account of a traveler who a few years ago journeyed through the interior of the State of Rio Grande do Sul:

> When I stopped for a short rest at a cottage on the way, almost the first act of the man who received me would be to charge his gourd with fresh powdered *mate*, then to fill it with the always ready boiling water, take a suck himself and then pass it to me; after I had sampled the decoction, the wife had her turn and all the other members of the family. To refuse to partake in this sincere act of welcome was to give offense, but I confess that it was unpleasant to put into my mouth the unclean tip of the pipe-like stem through which the *mate* drink was sucked. Except in these circumstances I grew to like *mate*, and even use it now, long after my return from South America. The old, old native keeps alive on *mate;* the German colonists find it good, and it displaces beer in their daily habits; the Italian settlers in the city or on the farm rapidly acquire the *mate* habit; the Spanish immigrant drops his high-priced wines and is as well satisfied with the nonalcoholic *yerba*, and even the north European peasant, beginning a strange life in this newest of new worlds, draws contentment and refreshment from this wonderful weed of South America.

Incidentally, it may be well to mention the fact that *yerba mate* may be prepared and consumed in a much more genteel fashion. The gourd is not at all a necessary adjunct, nor is the *bombilla*. It can be made in any teapot, and will taste just as good, if not better, when consumed like any other tea. The Germans in Curityba, and throughout Parana generally, prepare it by heating the water in a teapot to the boiling point, add a quantity of the powdered *mate*—

YERBA MATÉ READY FOR TRANSPORT.

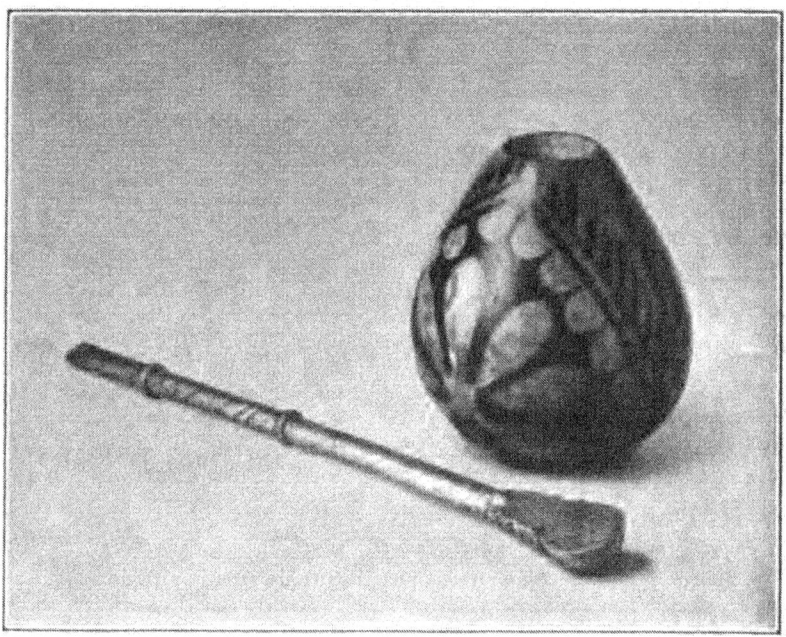

THE MATÉ AND THE BOMBILLA.

The maté is the usual name for the hollowed gourd from which the yerba maté (Paraguayan tea) is drunk. Colloquially, the word cuya is also frequently heard. The bombilla is the tube, of bone, reed, or metal (principally the last), through which the tea is sucked. The expanded end serves as a spoon, and the perforations in it are so small that the powdered leaves can not be drawn into the mouth. These utensils are sometimes made in very elaborate designs, and of precious metals.

A YERBA MATÉ CHUTE IN PARAGUAY.

Scenes like the above are frequently met with along the banks of the Paraguay River, where warehouses have been constructed on bluffs on the river bank and the yerba maté is collected awaiting the advent of the steamer. The densely packed hide sacks of maté are slid down the chute to the deck of the vessel, the work of loading being thus greatly minimized.

proportioned to suit the taste and strength desired—allow it to boil for a few moments, and then pour in sufficient cold water to stop the boiling and to settle the fine particles, much as coffee grounds are settled in boiling coffee, and the tea is then ready to be served in cups. Many persons add a little sugar, some even a small quantity of milk, but the inveterate *mate* drinker takes his straight.

This is the method of preparing the tea from the powdered product, the form in which it is usually found in the countries of its origin as well as in the comparatively few European and North American grocery establishments having it on sale. Recently, however, some enterprising Brazilian firms have placed a *yerba mate* extract, sweetened with sugar, on the market, and in this form it easily dissolves in either hot or cold water, and makes a beverage whose refreshing and stimulating qualities are remarkable. Lest the writer's estimate of the virtues of this harmless and yet invigorating drink be deemed exaggerated and biased the following paragraphs, taken from the work of the Rev. Dr. J. A. Zahm, C. S. C., Ph. D., entitled "Through South America's Southland," are herewith reproduced as being the opinion of a disinterested traveler who is as well known as a scientist as he is as an eminent divine:

This kind of *mate* is put up in small tin cans, and I am greatly surprised that it has not yet been introduced into the United States. I am convinced it would, as soon as known, become immensely popular. It is always ready for use and easily served. Besides this it has all the virtues of tea and coffee and none of their deleterious qualities. For persons of weak and delicate constitutions it is the most invigorating beverage imaginable and leaves no disagreeable after-effects. For use in hospitals it is invaluable. As a temperance drink it is nonpareil. It has preserved a large part of South America from the debasing evils of alcoholism, and I can conceive of no more powerful aid to the cause of temperance in our country than the popularizing of a beverage that has proved so efficacious among millions of people in our sister continent.

Chemists and physicians who have made a special study of the effects of *mate* on the human system are all loud in its praise. They recommend it both as a tonic and as a stimulant, and declare that it is destined to become a favorite prescription in hospitals for the sick and the convalescent. It is less of an excitant than tea or coffee. Unlike these two beverages, it does not cause insomnia, neither does it induce perturbations of the heart. It is the best substitute known for alcoholic drinks of all kinds and is particularly recommended to those who suffer from debility or neurasthenia.

But more conclusive as to its virtues than the experiments of physicians and chemists are the results that have attended its use for more than three centuries in South America. Where *mate* is used drunkenness is practically unknown. Among people like the Gauchos of Brazil and the Rio de la Plata region, where beef is the chief article of food, *mate* takes, to a great extent, the place of bread and vegetables. Give an Indian or a *caboclo*—the native Brazilian squatter—a handful of *mate* and he will row or work all day without food. It seems to dispel hunger and invigorate the body as effectually as coca. The best evidence as to its value as a tonic and as a substitute for solid food was furnished during the terrible war between Brazil and Paraguay nearly half a century ago. Then, writes the Brazilian general, Francisco da Rocha Callado, "I was witness during a period of 22 days, to the fact that our army was almost exclusively nourished by the *mate* which we collected in the *hervaes*, the lack of provisions on that occasion not permitting long halts." * * *

MEMBERS OF A RAILROAD CONSTRUCTION CAMP ENJOYING MATÉ.

Not only the natives of Paraguay and Brazil but thousands of European colonists are addicted to the use of yerba maté, and it is estimated that something like 15,000,000 people in South America habitually drink this delightfully stimulating beverage without incurring any of the ills attendant upon the use of alcoholic liquors.

So much for the unsolicited testimonial to *yerba mate* by the distinguished gentleman who was Col. Roosevelt's companion during his celebrated tour of South America in 1913. For the benefit of such food specialists as may desire to know something of the chemical constituents of the product as it is used in South America it may not be amiss to give the following table showing the component parts of *mate* as compared with tea (green and black) and coffee, on the authority of Dr. Caminhoa, professor of the faculty of medicine at Rio de Janeiro:

In 1,000 parts.	Green tea.	Black tea.	Coffee.	Mate.
Essential oil	7.90	6.00	0.41	0.01
Chlorophyl	22.20	18.14	13.66	62.00
Resin	22.20	36.40	18.66	20.69
Tannin	178.00	128.80	16.39	12.28
Theine or caffeine	4.30	4.60	2.66	2.50
Extract and coloring matter	464.00	390.00	270.67	238.83
Fibers and cellulose	175.80	283.20	174.83	180.00
Ash	85.60	54.40	25.61	38.10

Identically the same result is set forth in a comparative table made by Dr. Pekolt and indorsed by A. Moreau de Tours, analytical chemist of the Pasteur Institute of Paris.

From the above table it may be seen that *mate* contains much less of the essential oil than does either the green or black tea, and even less than coffee, and is consequently less of an excitant. It contains more of the resinous substance than does coffee, but less than the tea, and is therefore more diuretic than coffee and rivals tea in its stimulating qualities.

According to a recent report of United States Consul Maddin Summers, the price of *yerba mate*, f. o. b. Paranagua, Brazil, averages about 7 cents per pound, although there is some variation in the various grades, the finer qualities bringing from one-half to 1 cent per pound more than the average.

The use of this beverage, while almost unknown in the United States, is growing in popularity in Europe, the leading countries in the amounts imported prior to the breaking out of the war being Germany, France, and England in the order named. That it is not better known in this country is doubtless due to the fact that no systematic propaganda has been made to let the public know something of its excellent qualities. To the writer it would seem that the use of any harmless stimulant, that will in a measure take the place of the alcoholic beverages now consumed in such tremendous quantities, should be encouraged, and it is with the view of at least putting some small portion of the public on inquiry in regard to a drink which "cheers but does not inebriate" that this sketch has been prepared.

CPSIA information can be obtained at www.ICGtesting.com
Printed in the USA
BVOW09*2252100516

446751BV00018B/295/P